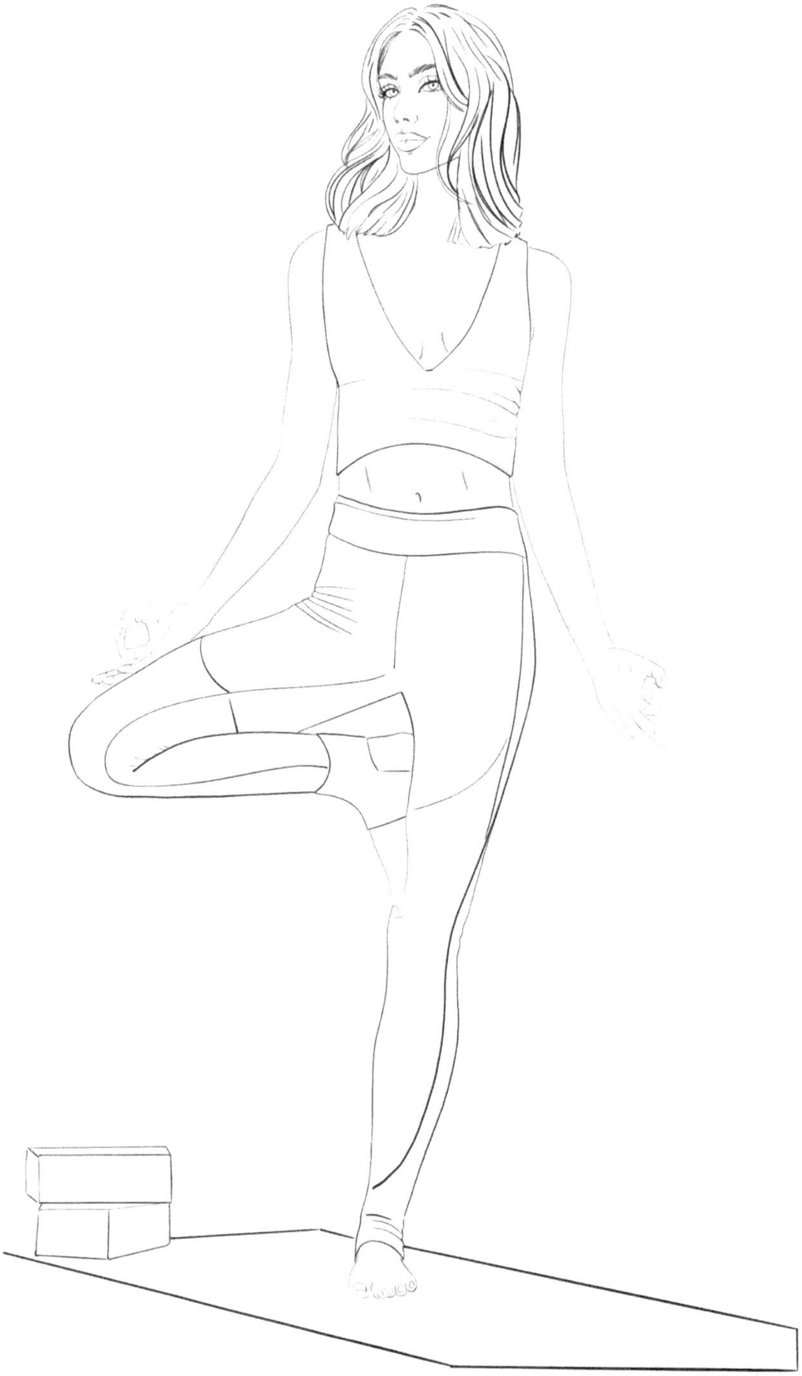

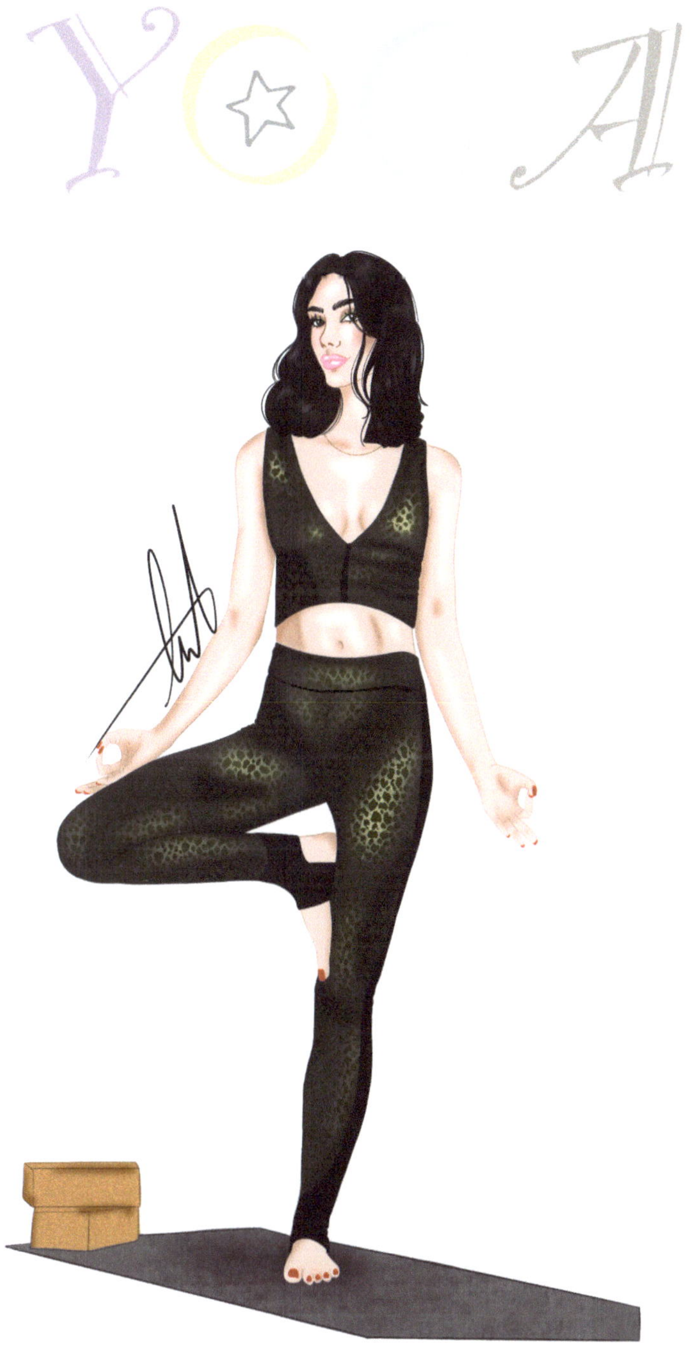
YO A

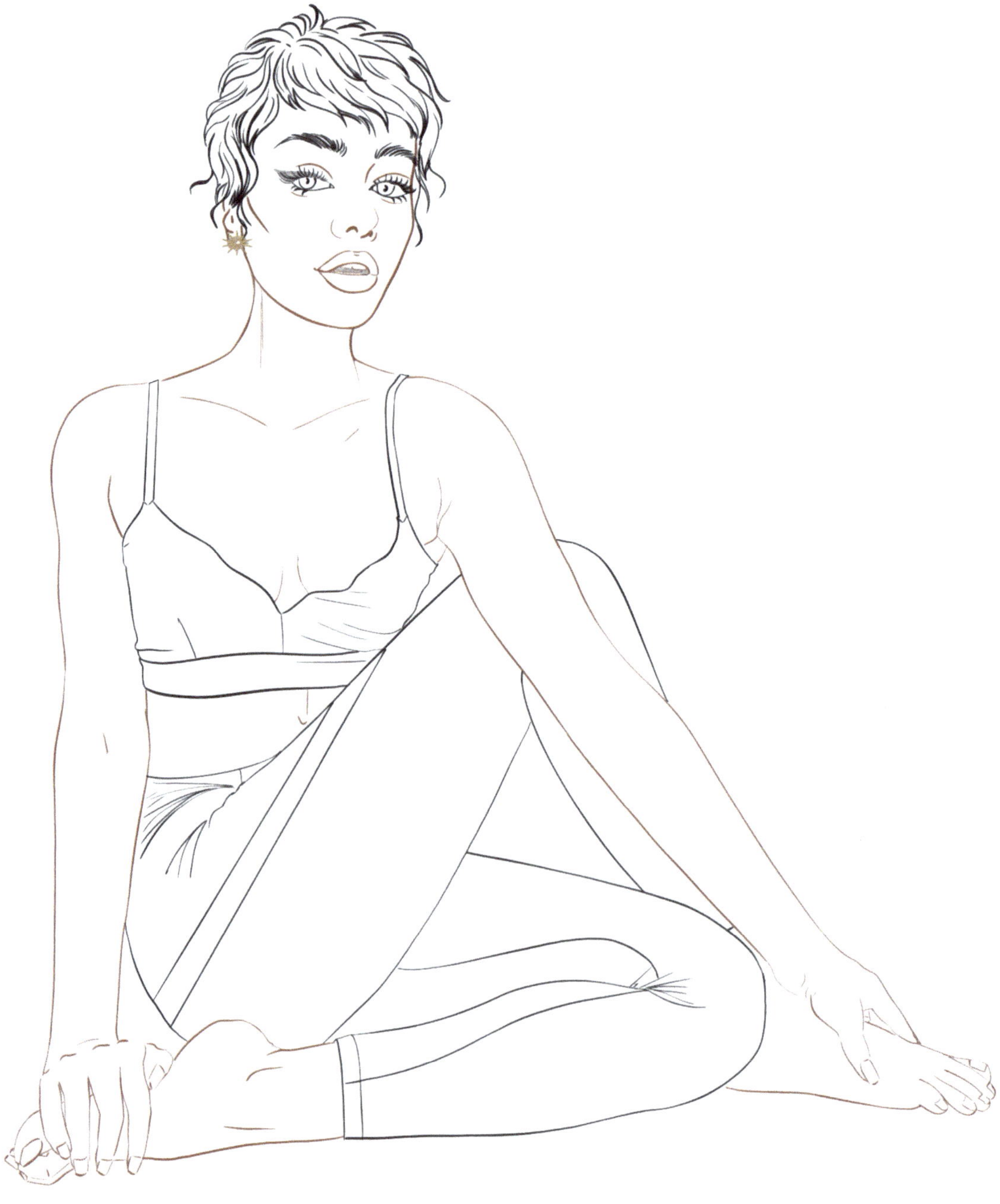

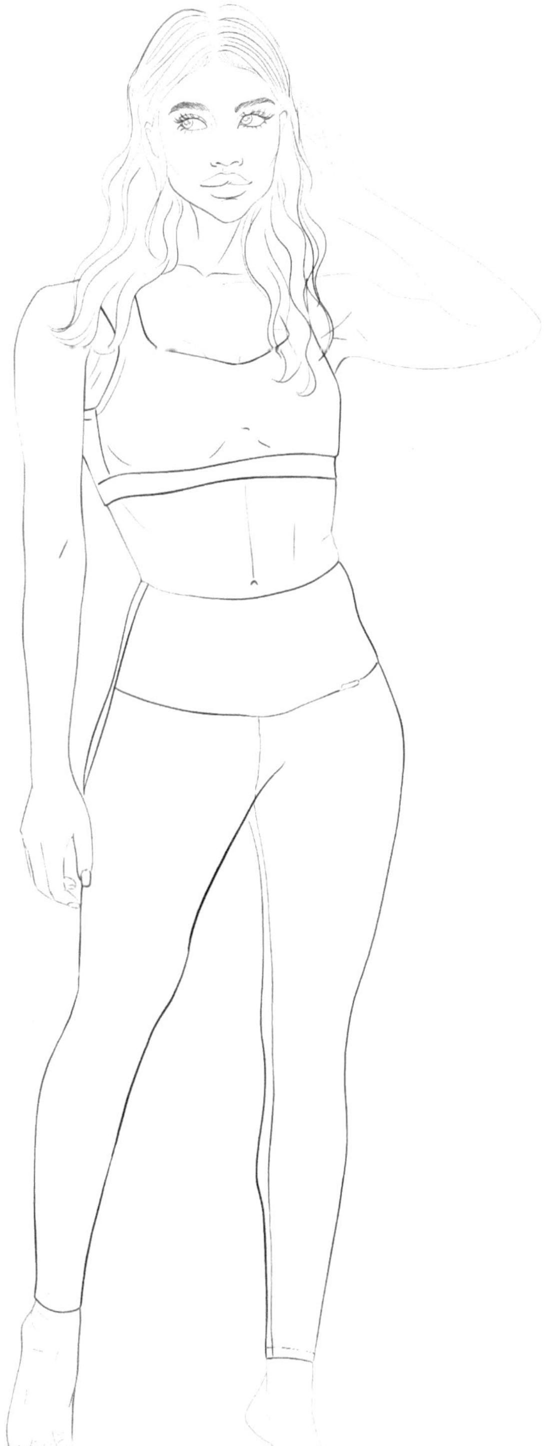

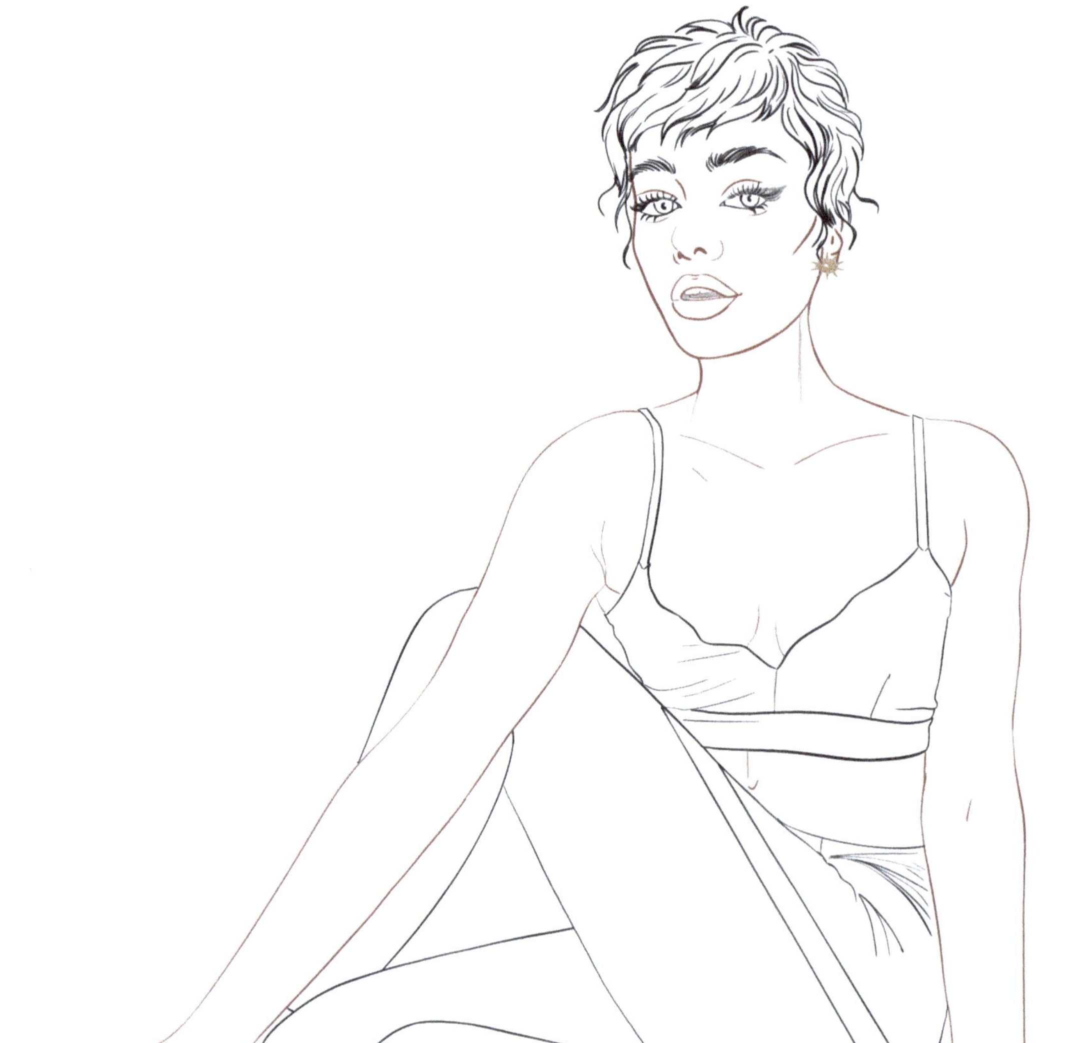

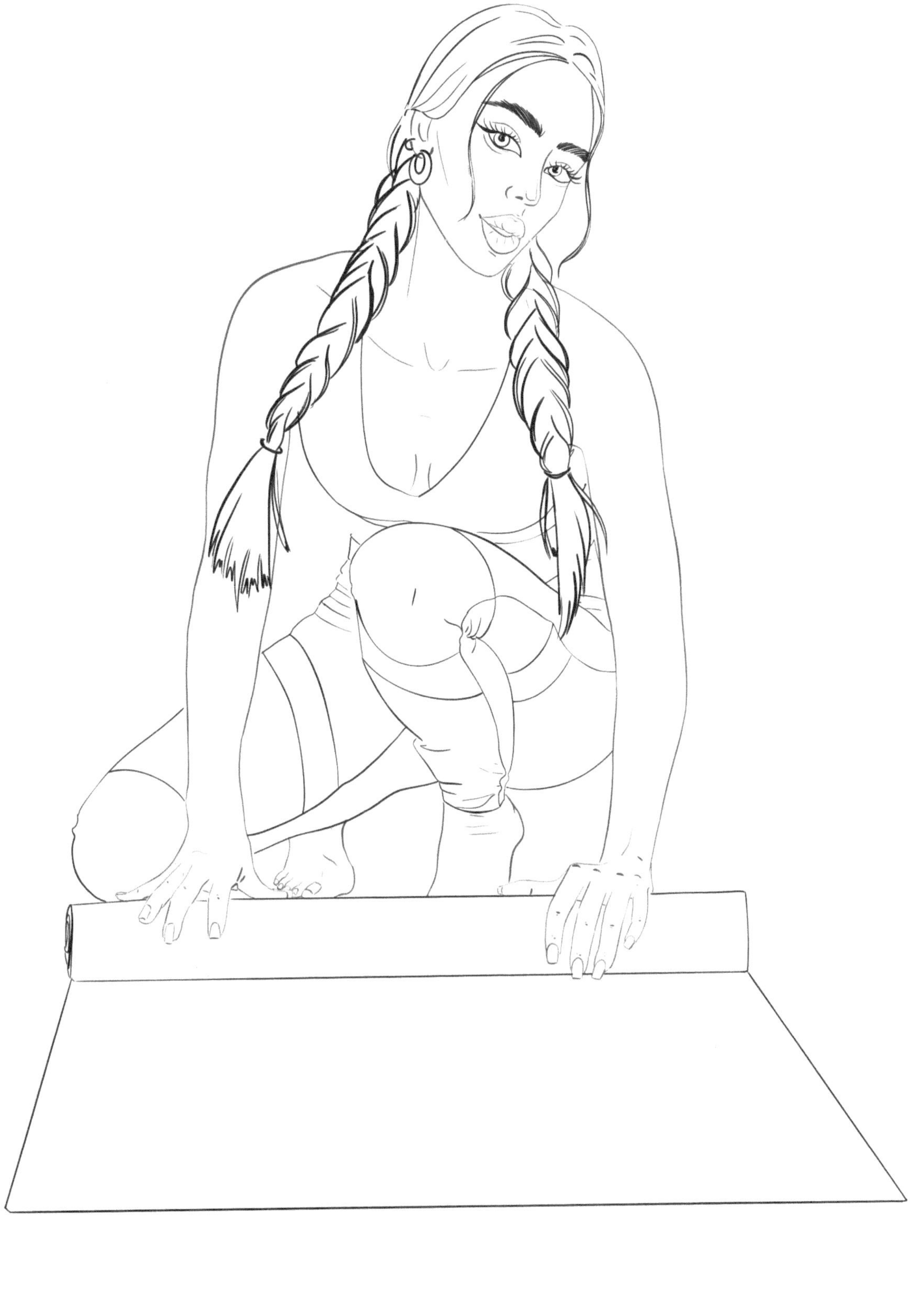

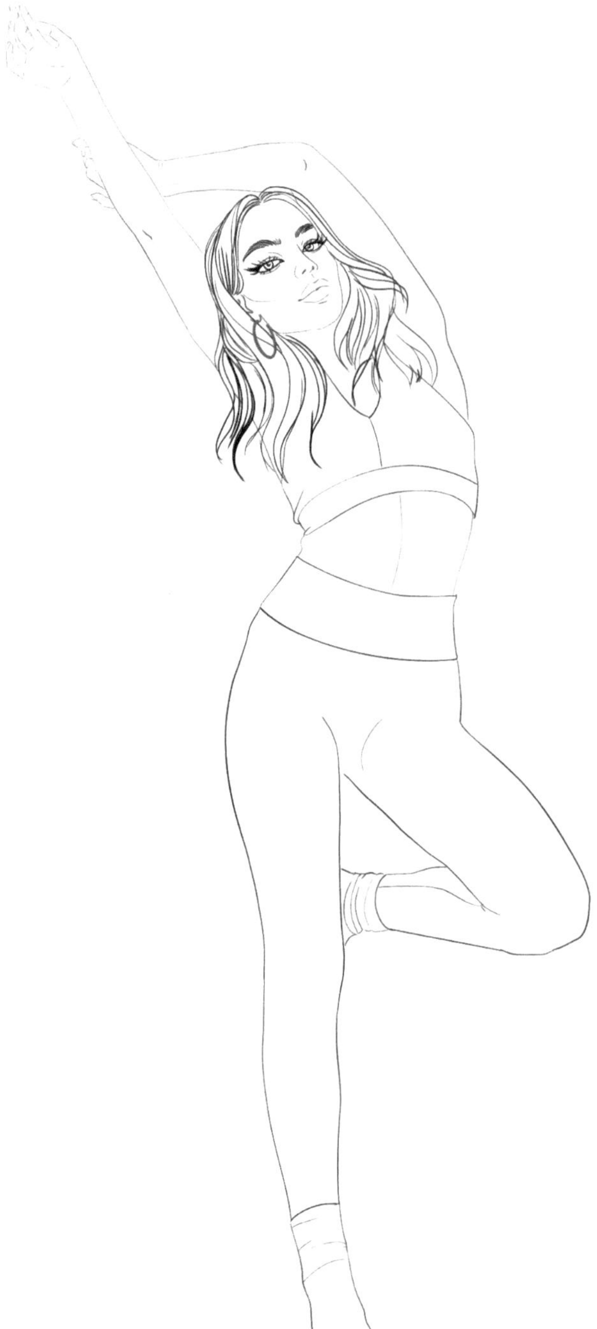

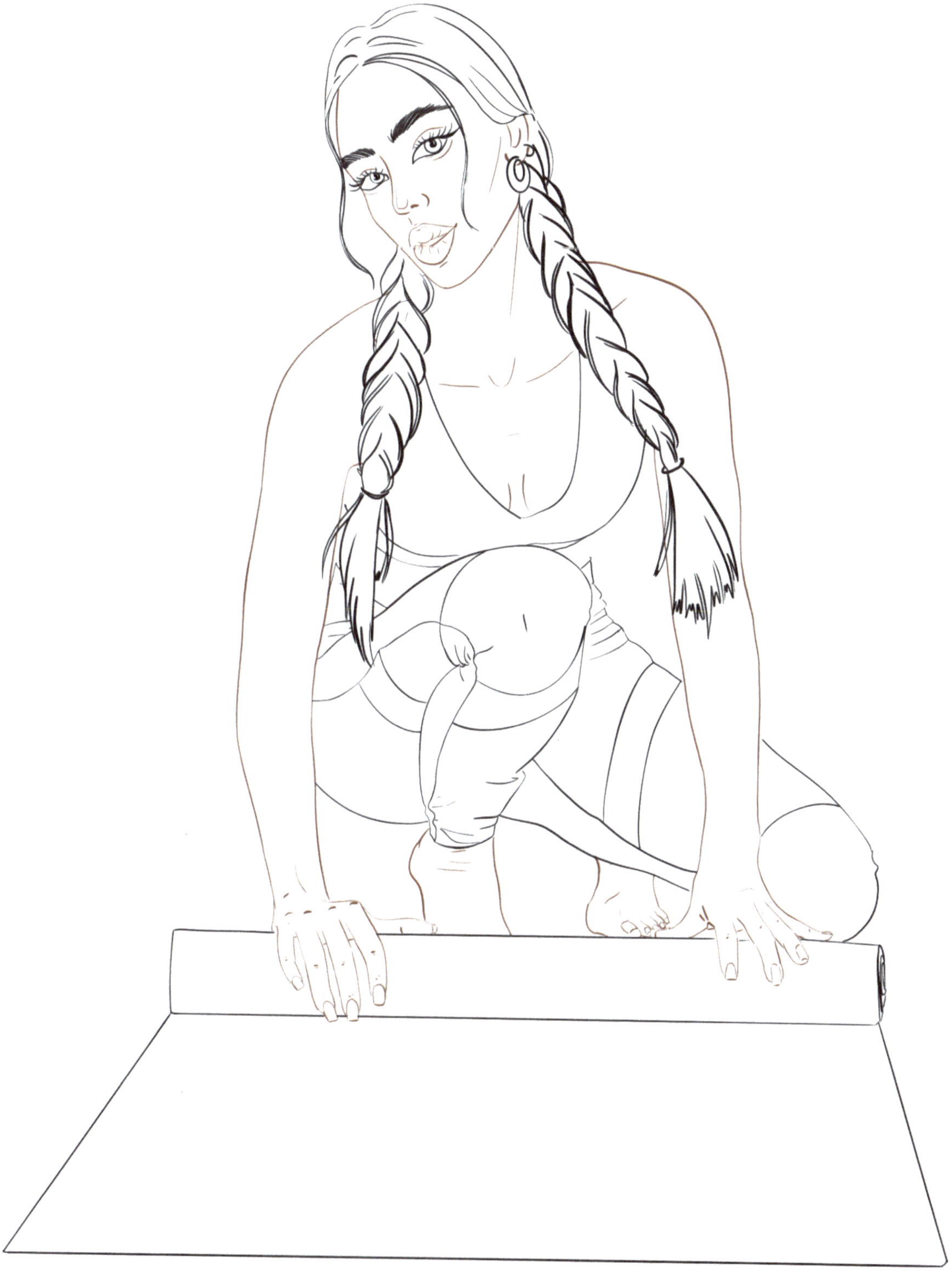

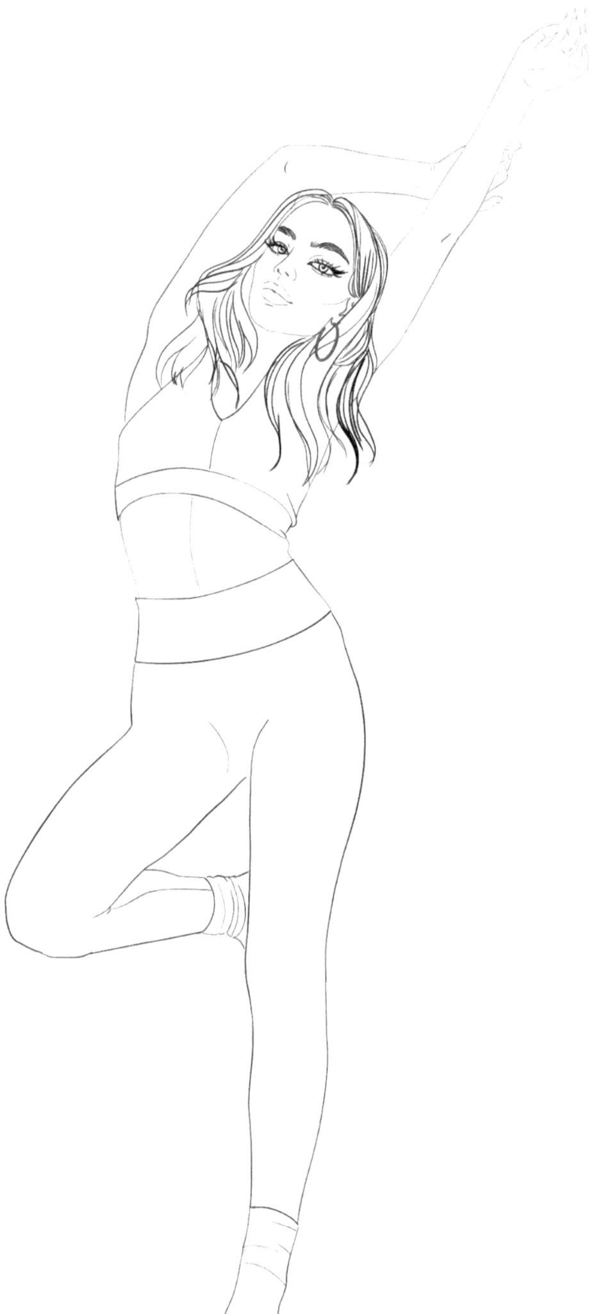

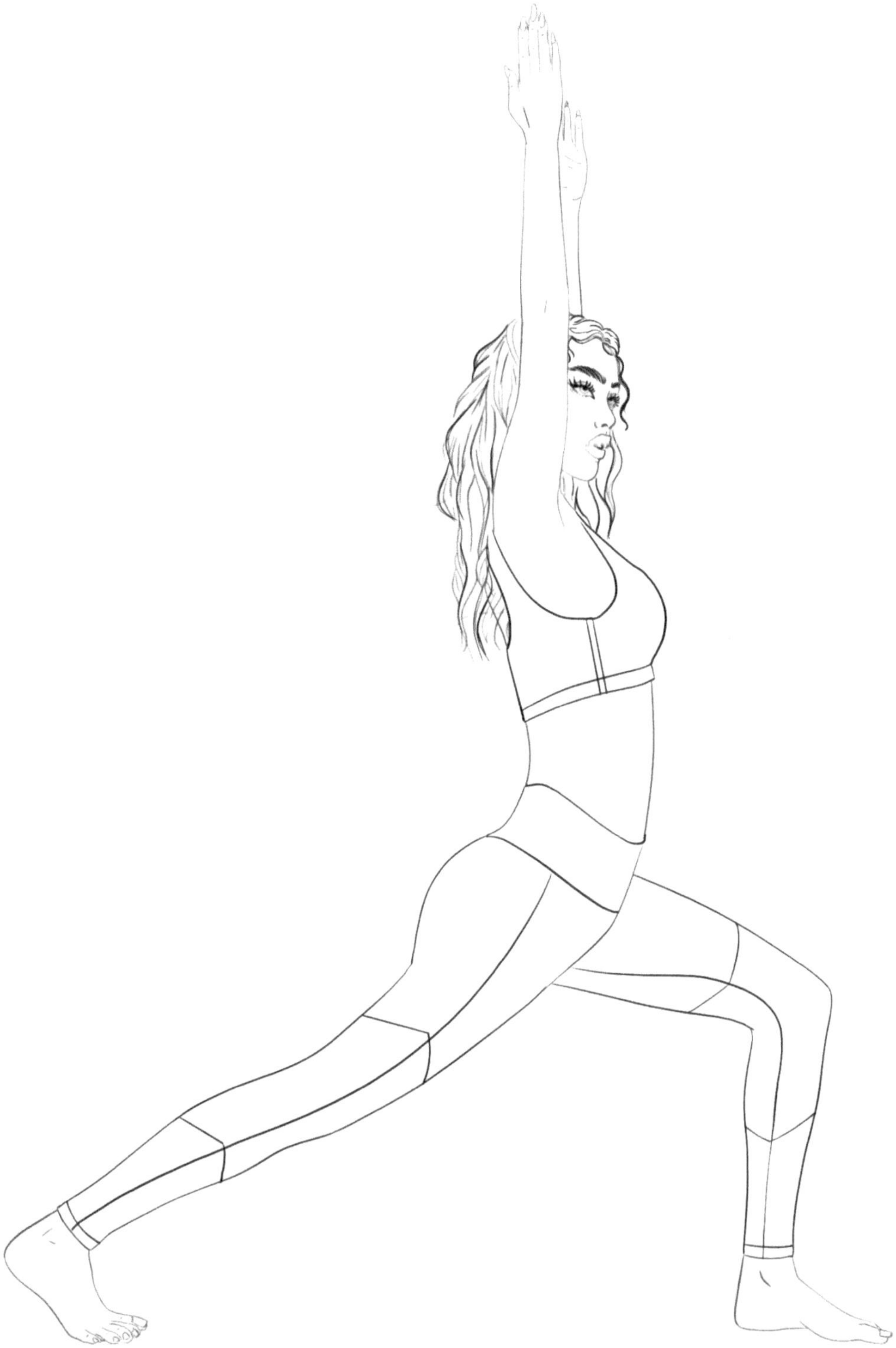

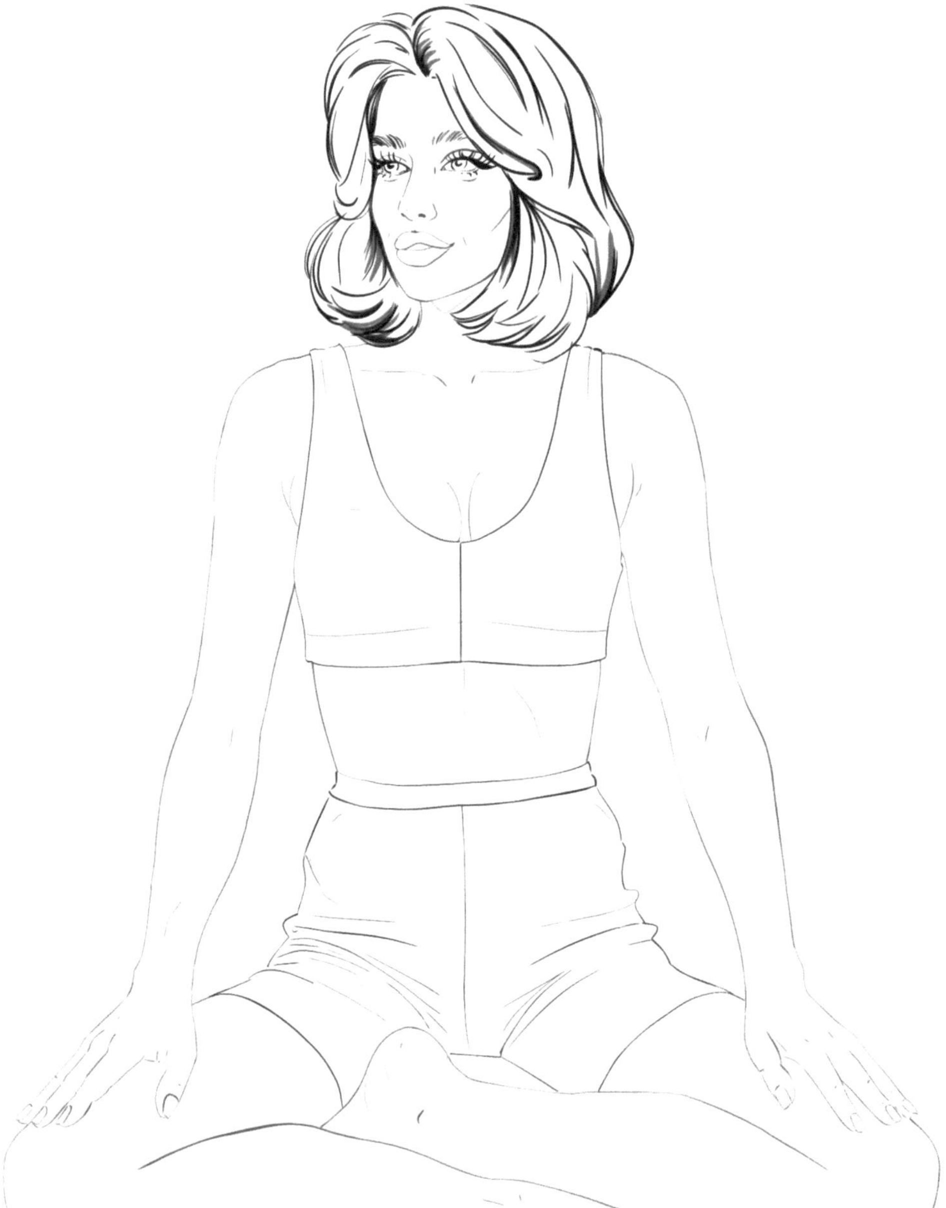

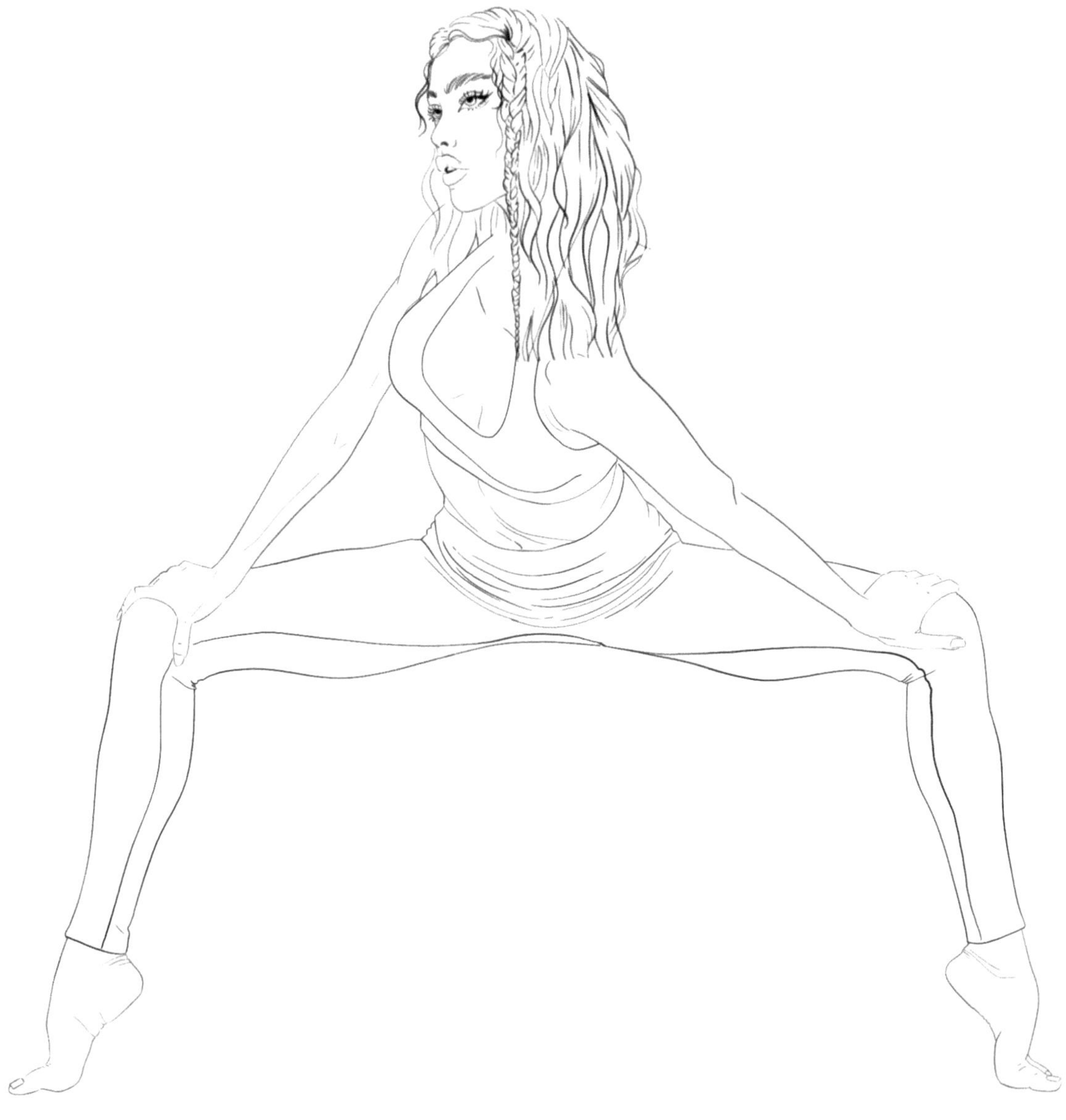

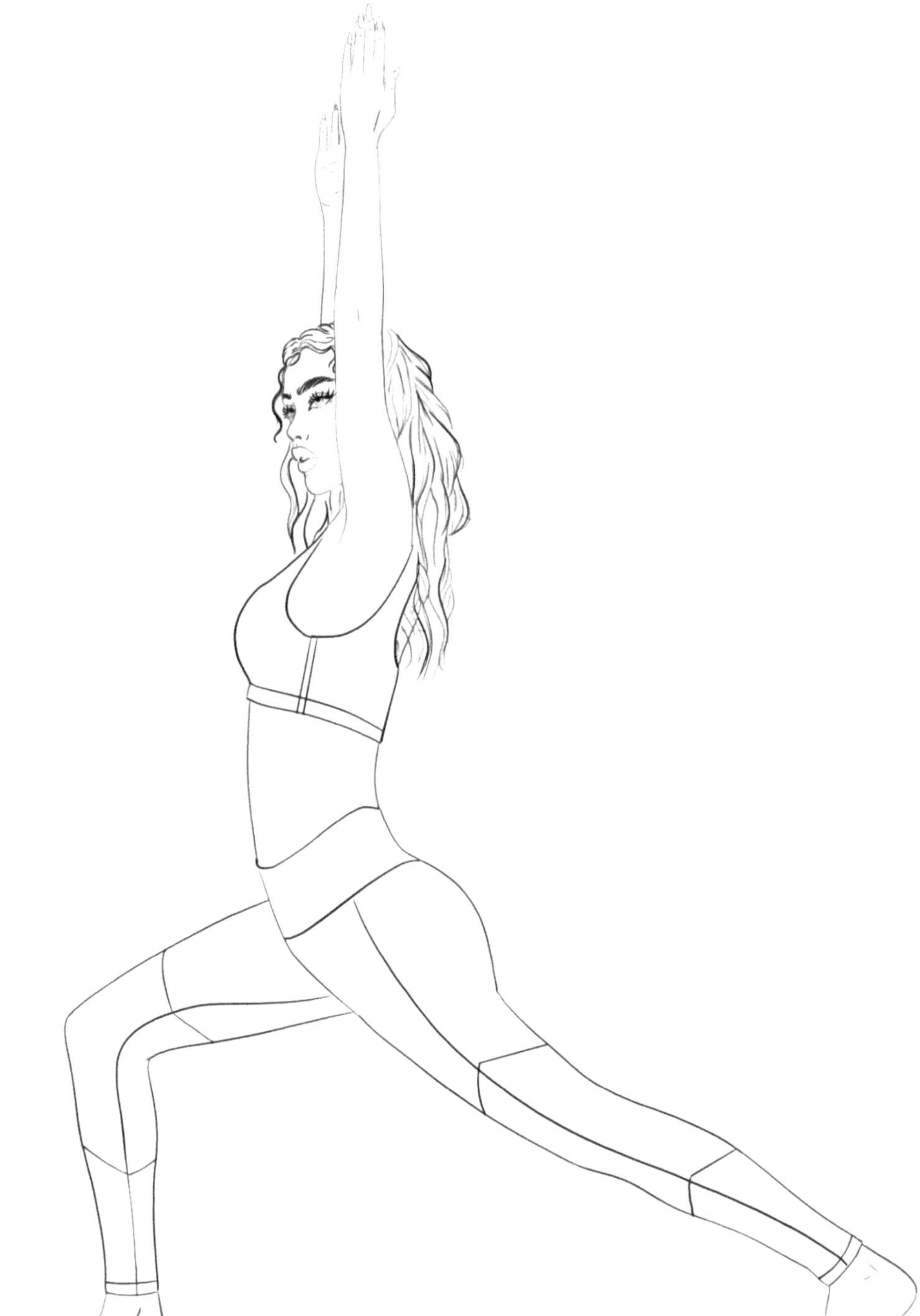

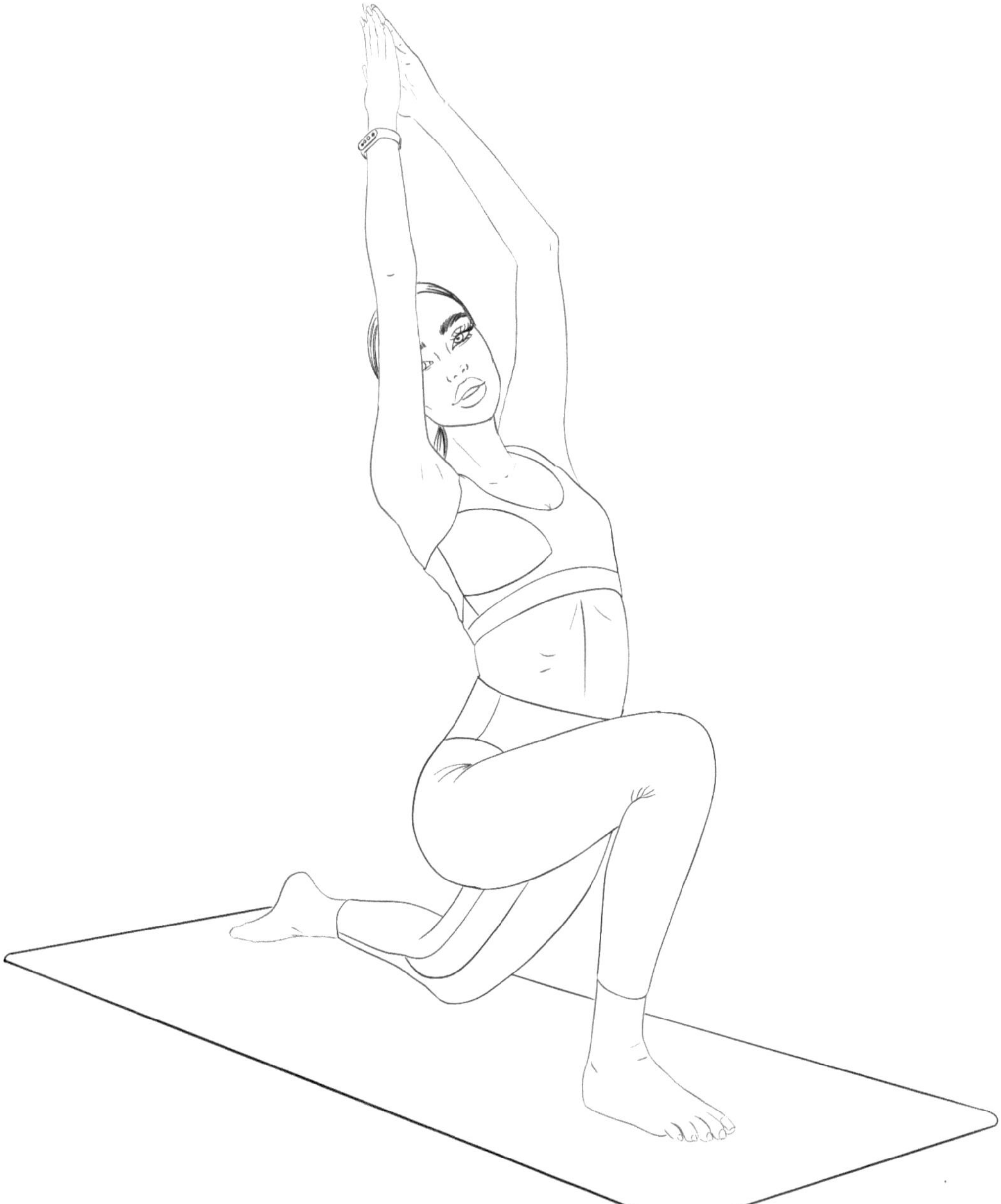

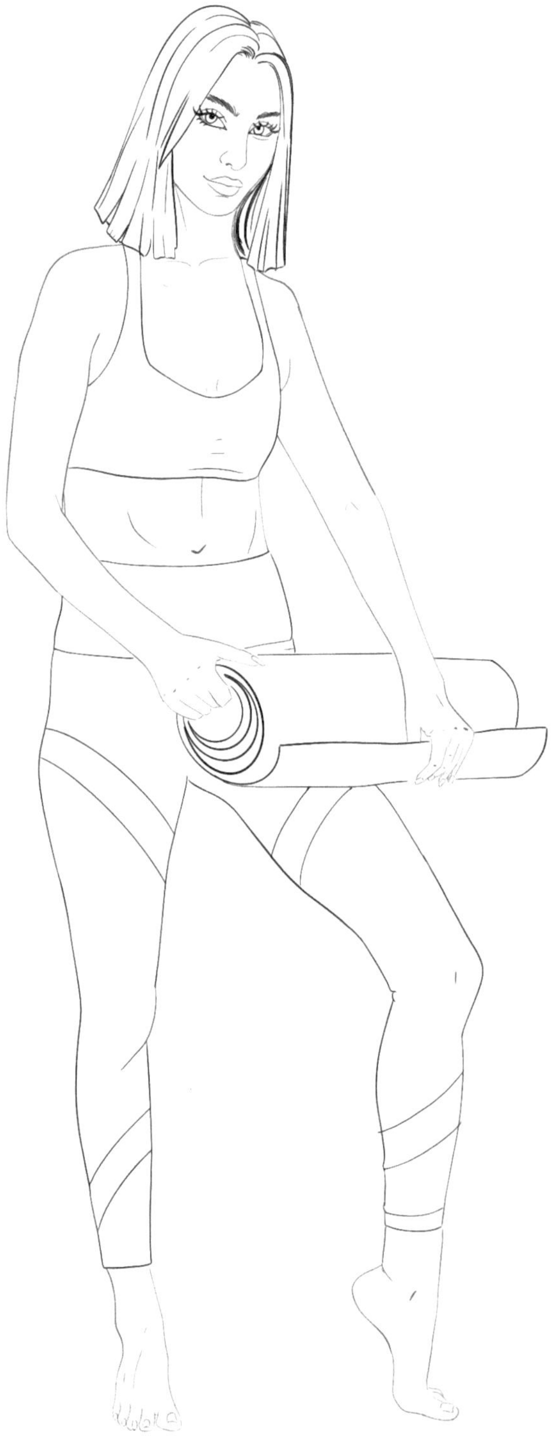

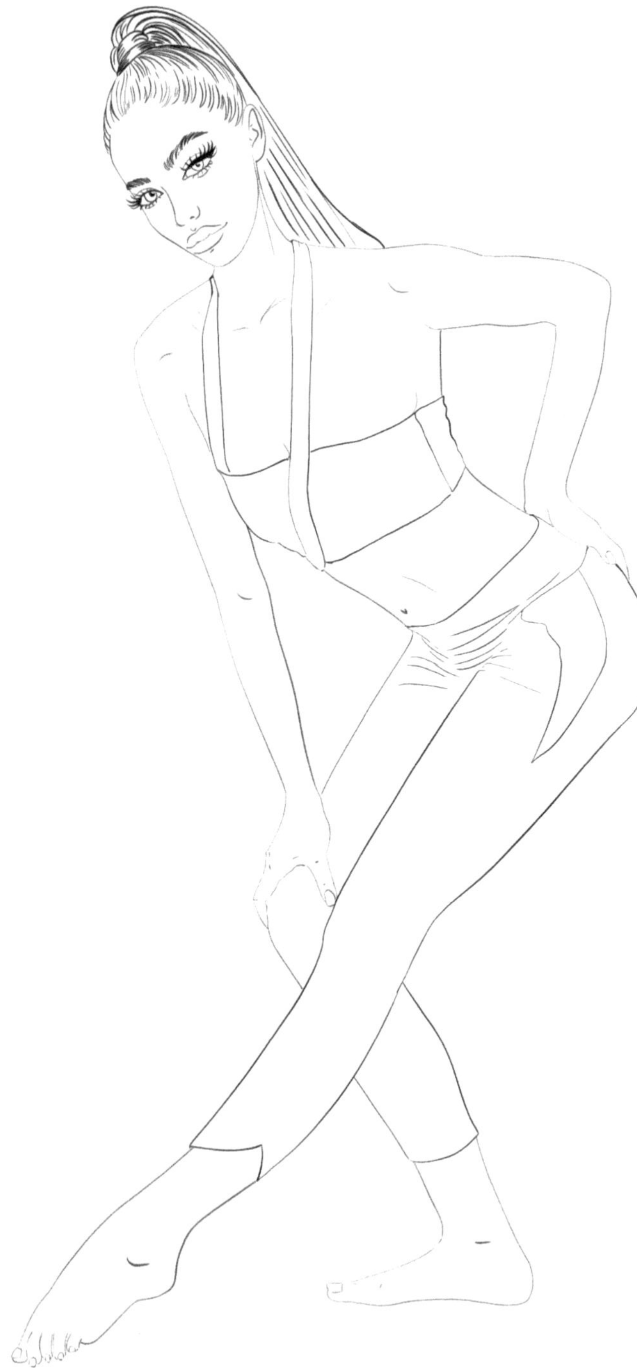

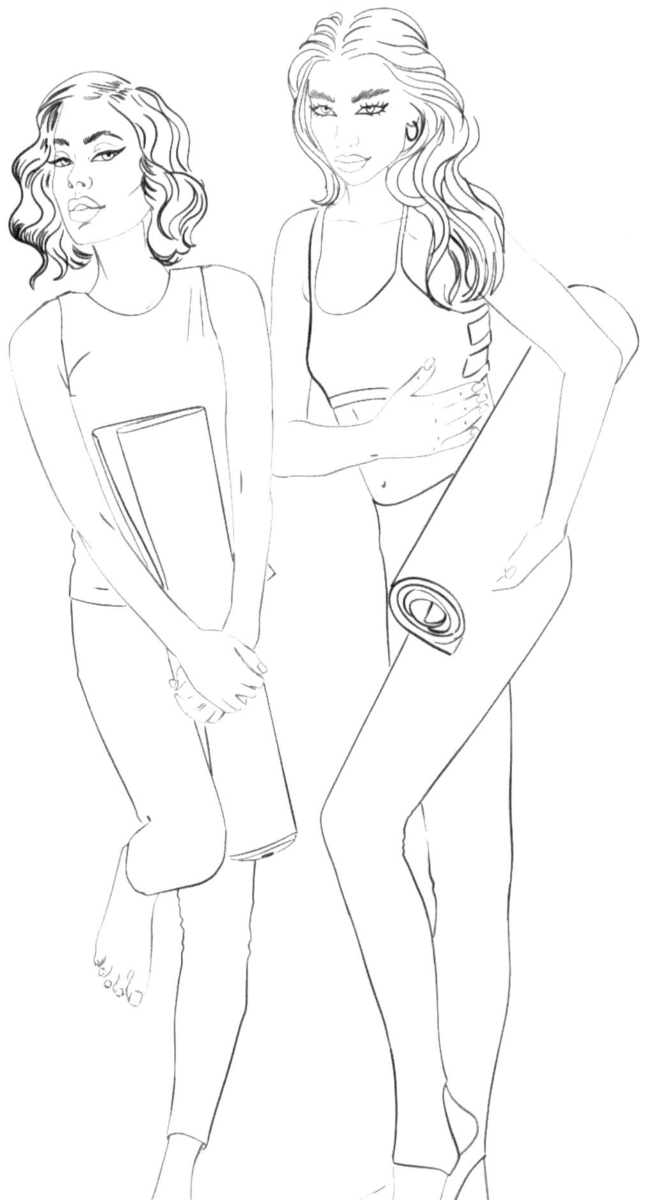

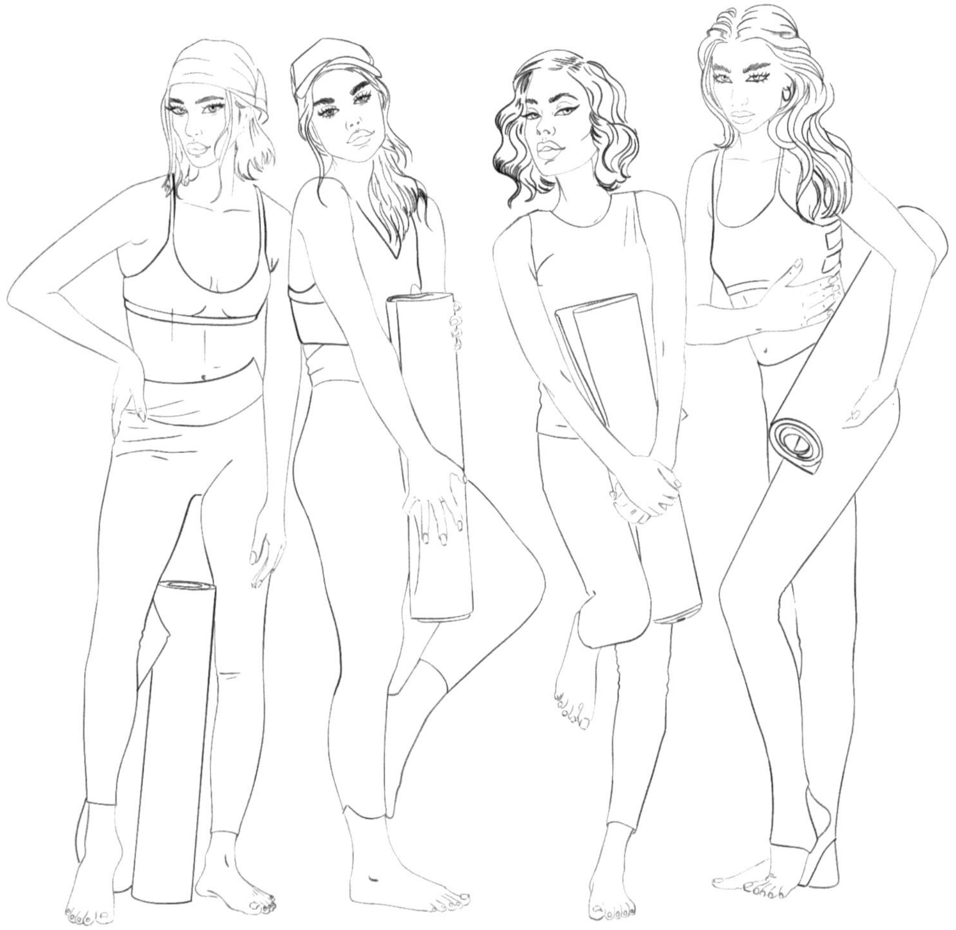

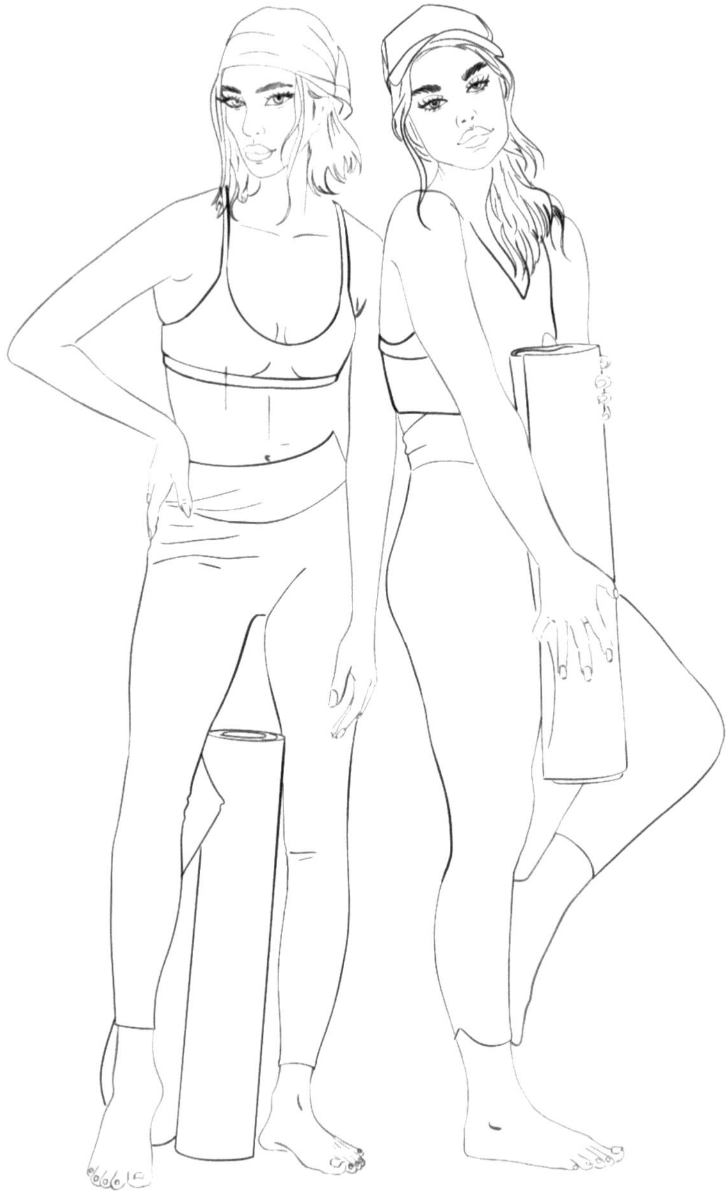

Color me

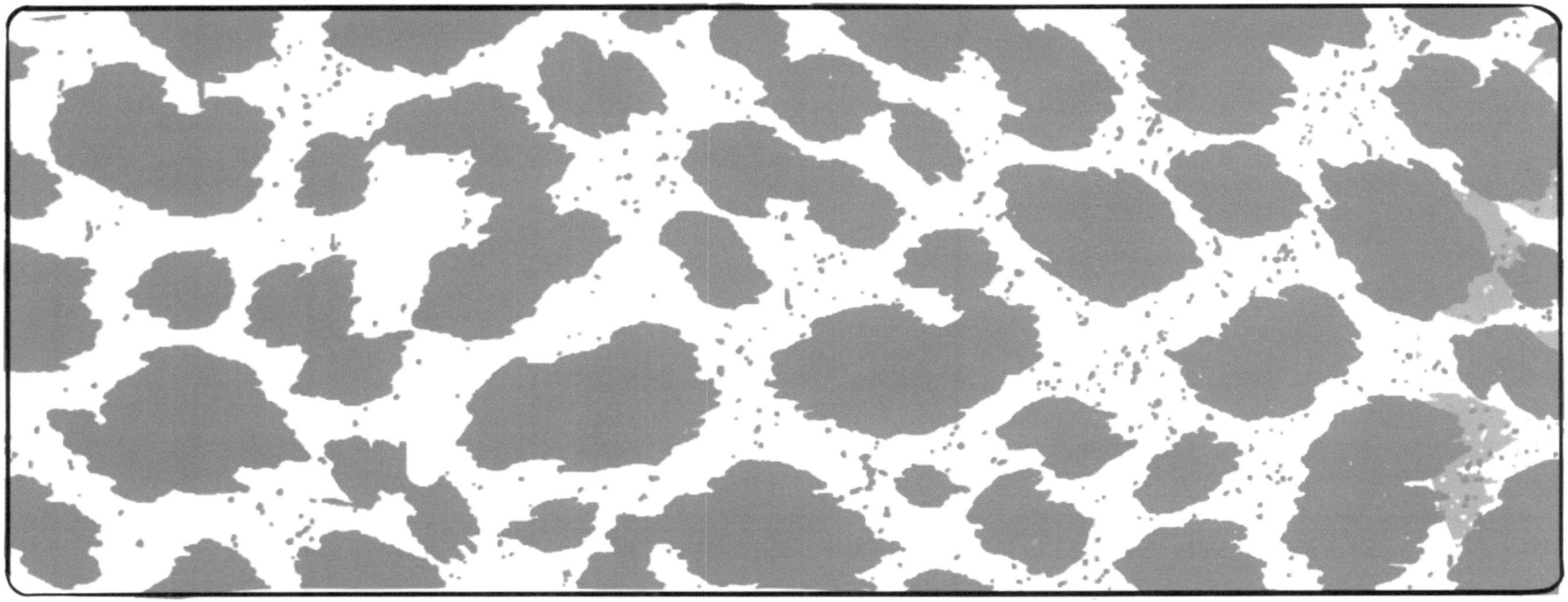

Color me

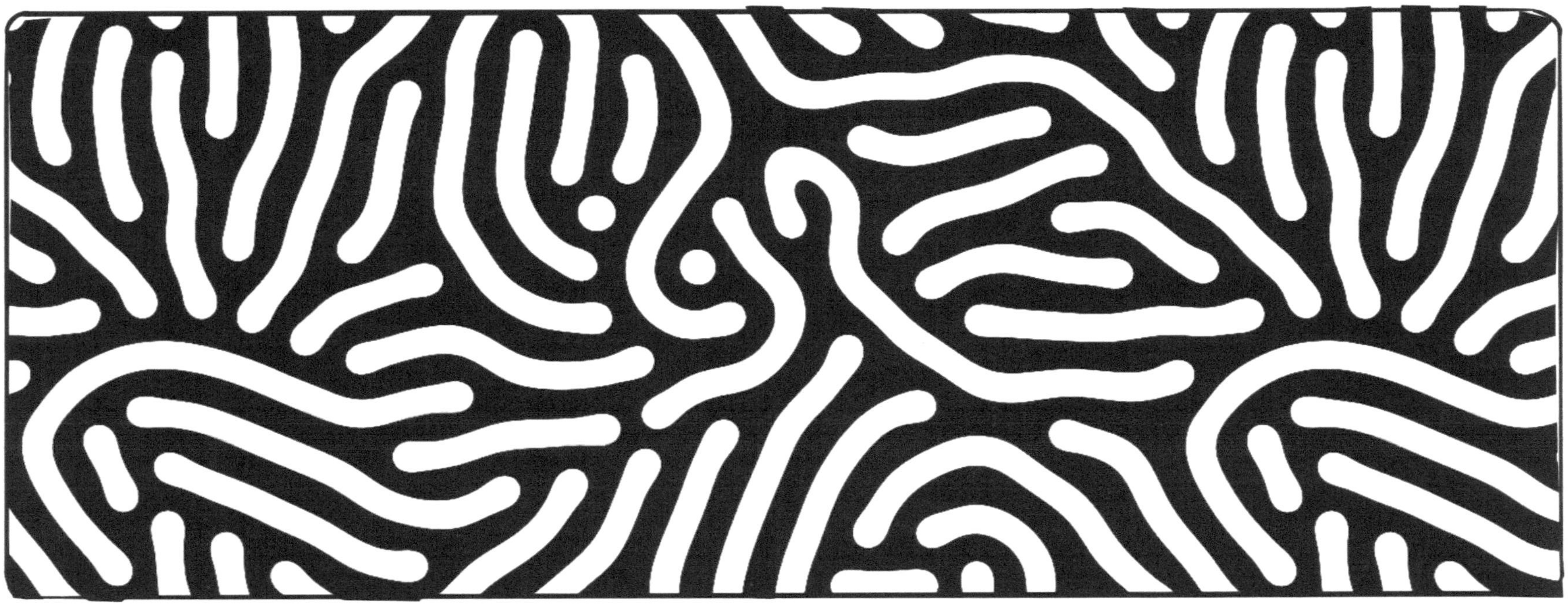

Color me

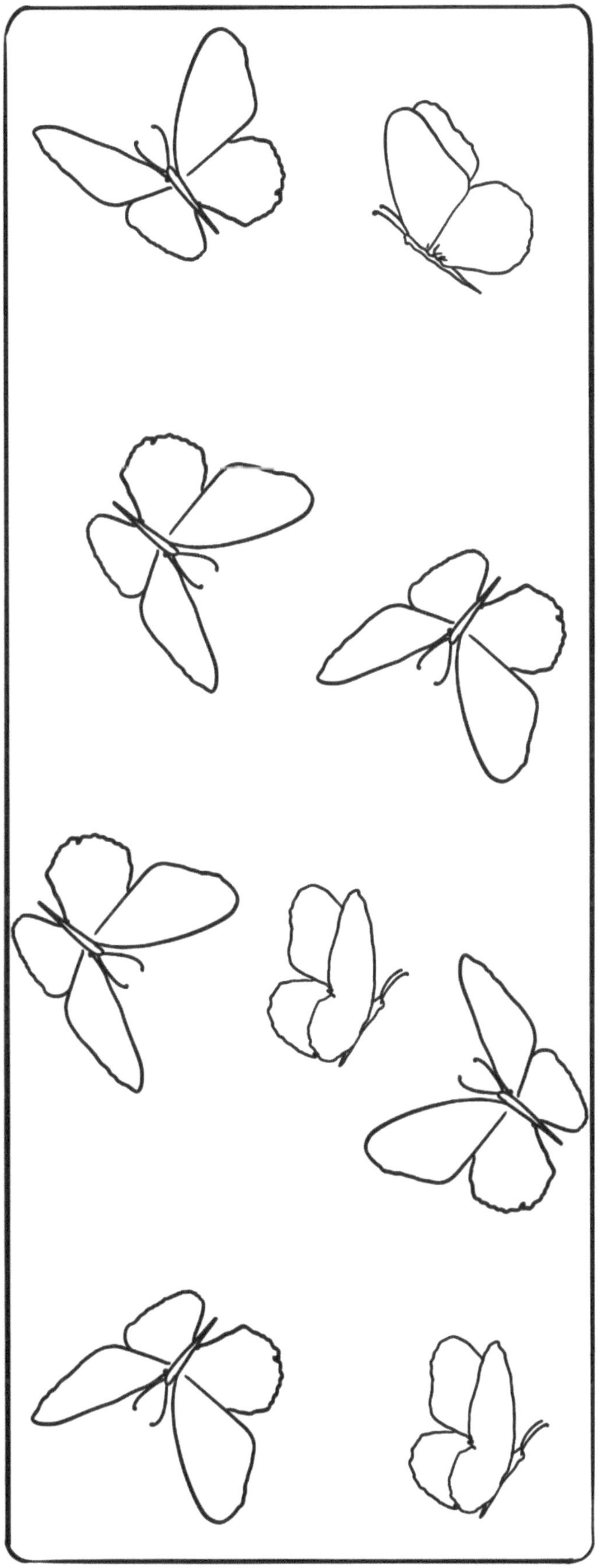

Color me

Create something here

www.ingramcontent.com/pod-product-compliance
Lightning Source LLC
Chambersburg PA
CBHW042029230526
45474CB00006B/61
* 9 7 9 8 3 2 5 1 6 9 9 3 9 *